HAL•LEONARD®
RECORDER
SONGBOOK

Disney HITS

The following songs are the property of:

Bourne Co.
Music Publishers
5 West 37th Street
New York, NY 10018

BABY MINE
WHISTLE WHILE YOU WORK

Disney characters and artwork © Disney Enterprises, Inc.

ISBN 978-1-4234-9301-3

WONDERLAND MUSIC COMPANY, INC.
WALT DISNEY MUSIC COMPANY

DISTRIBUTED BY

HAL•LEONARD®
CORPORATION

7777 W. BLUEMOUND RD. P.O. BOX 13819 MILWAUKEE, WI 53213

Visit Hal Leonard Online at
www.halleonard.com

BABY MINE

from Walt Disney's DUMBO

RECORDER

Words by NED WASHINGTON
Music by FRANK CHURCHILL

THE BARE NECESSITIES

from Walt Disney's THE JUNGLE BOOK

RECORDER

Words and Music by
TERRY GILKYSON

BIBBIDI-BOBBIDI-BOO
(The Magic Song)

from Walt Disney's CINDERELLA

RECORDER

Words by JERRY LIVINGSTON
Music by MACK DAVID and AL HOFFMAN

A DREAM IS A WISH YOUR HEART MAKES

from Walt Disney's CINDERELLA

RECORDER

Words and Music by MACK DAVID,
AL HOFFMAN and JERRY LIVINGSTON

Moderately, in 2

COLORS OF THE WIND

from Walt Disney's POCAHONTAS

Music by ALAN MENKEN
Lyrics bt STEPHEN SCHWARTZ

RECORDER

PART OF YOUR WORLD

from Walt Disney's THE LITTLE MERMAID

RECORDER

Music by ALAN MENKEN
Lyrics by HOWARD ASHMAN

REFLECTION

from Walt Disney Pictures' MULAN

Music by MATTHEW WILDER
Lyrics by DAVID ZIPPEL

RECORDER

SOMEDAY

from Walt Disney's THE HUNCHBACK OF NOTRE DAME

Music by ALAN MENKEN
Lyrics by STEPHEN SCHWARTZ

Recorder

A SPOONFUL OF SUGAR

from Walt Disney's MARY POPPINS

RECORDER

Words and Music by RICHARD M. SHERMAN
and ROBERT B. SHERMAN

WHEN SHE LOVED ME

from Walt Disney Pictures' TOY STORY 2 - A Pixar Film

RECORDER

Music and Lyrics by
RANDY NEWMAN

WHISTLE WHILE YOU WORK

from Walt Disney's SNOW WHITE AND THE SEVEN DWARFS

RECORDER

Words by LARRY MOREY
Music by FRANK CHURCHILL

ZIP-A-DEE-DOO-DAH

from Walt Disney's SONG OF THE SOUTH
from Disneyland and Walt Disney World's SPLASH MOUNTAIN

RECORDER

Words by RAY GILBERT
Music by ALLIE WRUBEL

WRITTEN IN THE STARS

from Elton John and Tim Rice's AIDA

RECORDER

Music by ELTON JOHN
Lyrics by TIM RICE

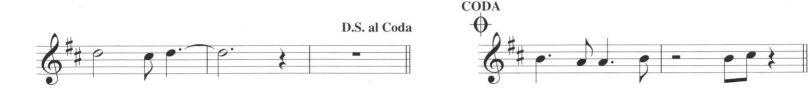

D.S. al Coda

CODA

YOU'LL BE IN MY HEART

(Pop Version)

from Walt Disney Pictures' TARZAN™

RECORDER

Words and Music by
PHIL COLLINS

YOU'VE GOT A FRIEND IN ME

from Walt Disney's TOY STORY

RECORDER

Music and Lyrics by
RANDY NEWMAN